The Princess
of Cyres Hill

The Princess of Cyres Hill

Pamela McGee Wilkinson

The Princess of Cyres Hill

Copyright © 2025 by Pamela McGee Wilkinson

ISBN: (Paperback)   978-1-967279-43-2
             (Hardback)   978-1-967279-44-9
             (eBook)   978-1-967279-45-6

Blue Ink Media Solutions
1111B S Governors Ave
STE 7582 Dover,
DE 19904
www.blueinkmediasolutions.com

This book is dedicated to Emma Ethel Powell McGee.

A nurse and the poet laureate of the hospital in Columbia, Louisiana circa 1940s to 1960s. Emma was my grandmother, my father's mother, and besides her amazing southern chicken and dumplings that she shared during our visits to her home, she shared her poetry. She never had to get out a copy of the poems as she knew them all by heart. I would sit on her bed along with my siblings, Mike, Bobbie, Pat and Mark as she quoted poem after poem. I loved her style and thought that it was amazing that she could make words rhyme so perfectly and inject the right amount of humour. Years later, I copied her style and therefore dedicate this book to her legacy.

Thanks Gee Gee for the poetry and the dumplings.

Emma was asked to write a poem for a very portly doctor who had to have his clothes specially made due to his weight. They wanted to present him a pair of slacks for a Christmas present to him from the hospital staff.

The Christmas Slacks
by Emma Powell McGee

You should have heard Old Santy's language
as we gave him the dimensions of those slacks
The wires from the North Pole were trembling
when these words were coming back.

"Now you know you must be jestin'.
This is bound to be a fake
For you must own a circus
and a tent you want to make."

It's no joke dear Old Santy.
That much cloth you've got to git
For our doctor must have britches
and they really ought to fit.

"Goodness gracious! said Old Santy
Don't this doctor have apparel?
My cloth must be divided
Can't you put him in a barrel?"

Oh no dear! That would be so awful
Gettin' in and out of cars
When his patients saw him coming
They would think he came from Mars.

"Well, I'll get them out real early
And I hope they fit quite well
But I'll throw away the dimensions
and I'll never ever tell.

Because Christmas is a time for giving.
I guess this fact I'll have to face.
Ain't no use for me to worry
if all my cloth is going to one place."

PREFACE

In 2000 and 2001 my oldest daughter and her husband lived in Newton St. Cyres near Exeter, England where he pursued a degree in Shakespearean works. Along with this ambitious couple was their two young daughters, Hana and Emma, Hana being the oldest at about 2½ years.

Living in America at the time, fairly expensive phone calls from Louisiana to Newton St. Cyres were short and sweet. I vividly remember having a short conversation with Hana toward the end of 2000. It had been a few months since we had spoken privately and during that conversation I was taken aback. I tried to listen to her telling me some exciting news for a 2½ year old but found it difficult to understand her. When she had finished her story she handed the phone to her mother who was sitting nearby.

I asked my daughter what had happened to her voice and she said "Oh that. She's picked up a British accent from her nursery school friends." Indeed she had! I thought about that tiny little American girl who now sounded British a lot after that conversation and called her "my tiny English princess".

Not too long after that call, I received in the mail a postcard from my daughter of a map of Great Britain. As soon as I had it in my hands and gazed at it a few seconds, I instantly sensed or visualized my tiny English princess, but now a pre-pubescent maid, roaming the southwestern part of England in the days of yore. Her joy and energy coupled with her grace and a royal bloodline were evident to all who laid eyes on her. She was a delight to watch as she travelled the countryside on her favorite horse. In my mind, she was so unforgettable that she was pleasantly remembered for hundreds and hundreds of years in Devonshire. Like King Arthur, the locals loved whispering rumors about her life and travels throughout their countryside.

This vision of my tiny princess and this very tangible postcard inspired this poem. It was written with pen and paper in less than two hours. Twenty years later, I have become obsessed with making this poem a children's book for young girls and boys who still believe in princes and princesses. A poetic gift that was written for my first grandchild is now available to all who enjoy reading about royalty… even if it may be fictional. Enjoy.

Pamela McGee Wilkinson

The Princess of Cyres Hill

IN NEWTON ST. CYRES
A FAR AWAY PLACE
THERE LIVED A TINY PRINCESS
FULL OF JOY AND FULL OF GRACE

HER SMILE WAS LIKE THE MORNING
HER HAIR WAS SUNSET SPUN
HER EYES WERE POOLS OF AMBER
HER COUNTENANCE THE SUN

SHE DRESSED IN IVORY LINENS
WOVE RIBBONS THROUGH HER HAIR
PLACED LACE AND SATIN SLIPPERS
ON PRECIOUS FEET AND FAIR

HER MIND WAS FILLED WITH WONDER
HER HEART WOULD WAX WITH PRIDE
FOR SHE WAS A PRINCESS OF CYRES
AND THE ROYALS OF MCBRIDE

EACH DAY THAT DRIFTED BY
AND EACH SUN THAT WOULD SET
IMOGEN RULED HER LAND
WITHOUT SADNESS OR REGRET

SHE WAS STEADFAST AND LOYAL
TO HER HERITAGE, TO HER NAME
SHE LOVED FAMILY AND FRIENDS
AND COUNTRYMEN JUST THE SAME

SHE LOVED THE LANDS OF CYRES
FROM SEAS TO MOUNTAIN PEAKS
SHE GAZED UPON THEIR BEAUTY
AND FOUND IT HARD TO SPEAK

EVERY ANIMAL, EVERY BIRD
WERE OH SO PRECIOUS AND DEAR
AS EVERY TREE AND EVERY BUSH
EVERY BLOSSOM THAT WOULD APPEAR

SHE SMELLED OF LILAC BLOSSOMS
THAT SHE PICKED FROM CYRES HILL
TOWERING NEAR THE CRAGGY ROCKS
ALONG A BABBLING RILL

SHE GATHERED BUNDLES OF HEATHER
ALONG THE CASTLE PATH
AND SPRINKLED FRAGRANT PETALS
IN EACH AND EVERY BATH

SHE FROLICKED IN THE GARDENS
SHE DANCED IN THE RAINS
SHE RODE HER HORSE THROUGH ENGLISH WOODS
AND SKIPPED DOWN COUNTRY LANES

SHE FOUND FOUR LEAF CLOVERS
ON WARM AND WINDY DAYS
SHE BATHED IN DEVON PONDS
AND SLEPT ON BRISTOL HAYS

SHE KNEW THE LANDS OF CORNWALL
SHE SWAM NEAR THURLESTONE ROCKS
SHE PICKED WILD BERRIES NEAR THE TOWNS
OF DEVONPORT, OF PLYMSTOCK

SHE WALKED THE ANCIENT MOORS
AND DREAMT OF DAYS OF YORE
OF KNIGHTS IN SHINING ARMOUR BRIGHT
ALONG THE DARTMOUTH SHORE

HER BEAUTY AND HER MAJESTY
WERE TALKED OF LANDS ABROAD
SHE WAS THE FINEST MAID TO WALK
ON ANY ENGLISH SOD

HER ROYAL NOBLE BIRTHRIGHT
GAVE HONOR TO HER NAME
IN NEWTON ST. CYRES
YOU'LL HEAR THE LOCALS CLAIM

THAT ALL ALONG THE COUNTRY PATHS
AND IN THE VALLEYS STILL
YOU'LL HEAR THE LAUGHTER OF THE MAID
WHO PLAYED ON CYRES HILL